HOLLYWOOD

JOUR

HOLLYWOOD

JOUR

L O S T

R E C I P E S

O F L E G E N D A R Y

H O L L Y W O O D

H A U N T S

•

Betty Goodwin

Design by Jeff Darnall

ANGEL CITY PRESS

ANGEL CITY PRESS INC.

Published by Angel City Press

2210 Wilshire Boulevard, Suite 880

Santa Monica, California 90403

(310) 395-9982

First published in 1993 by Angel City Press

3 5 7 9 10 8 6 4

Copyright © Betty Goodwin 1993

Library of Congress Catalog Card Number: 93-71393

ISBN 1-883318-22-X

Printed in the United States of America

To my parents

ACKNOWLEDGMENTS

*D*ad gave Mom her engagement ring over lunch at La Rue. I was fortunate to come along later and be squired to all the best restaurants. Fast forward a few years, and my special restaurant friends Joan and Bill Luther and Burks Hamner eased my transition from mere diner-outer into cookbook author. I was aided in my research and detective work by Romaine Ahlstrom and Dan Strehl of the Los Angeles Public Library, Stacey Behlmer and Sandra Archer at the Academy of Motion Picture Arts and Sciences' Margaret Herrick Library, the California Restaurant Association's Stanley Kyker and Bob Riley, Kurt Niklas, Richard Gully, Margaret Burk, Lois Dwan, Robert Cohn, Marty Mills, Cheryl Crane, Josh LeRoy, Marlene Morris, Tom and Sandy Sturges, David Price, Marc Wanamaker, Joe Stellini, Evelyn Lane Dankner, Patti Black, Lynn Bergeron, Milton Weiss, Silvio Petoletti, Valli Zale, Shirley Wilson, Katie Whitehead, Helen Chaplin and Ron Haver. I owe much gratitude to Jeff Silverman, Ina Chow, Kathy St. Ives at the *Los Angeles Times* and Alan and Alex Berliner for their kind assistance and generosity. Lastly, haloes to my four "Angels" at the Press – Paddy Calistro, Jean Penn, Scott McAuley and Neil Feineman.

Betty Goodwin
Beverly Hills, California

Contents

Introduction

*G*reat restaurants are said to be like theater – the mood, the backdrop and the star players mean as much as the food on the plate. Well, in Hollywood those qualities are magnified dramatically, for no one understands production qualities better than they do in the birthplace of the movies.

Since the twenties – concurrent with the development of talkies – many of the community's most legendary restaurants sprung up as colorfully as the larger-than-life personalities who frequented them. The tales behind the owners themselves (often rags-to-riches stories) rivaled the plots of any film – the gambler who bet his money on a Polynesian paradise and won, the ersatz Russian prince who ran one of the toniest spots in town, the distinguished movie director whose restaurant fantasies matched his on-screen oeuvre.

On a rudimentary level, Hollywood restaurants were born the minute somebody felt hunger pangs. But ever since press agents sent stars into the night dutifully glossed and groomed to be photographed with their escort of the moment, restaurant-going took on a function more important than mere nourishment. Being seen in the right place was work for the town's movers and shakers, and still is.

Hollywood and its restaurants thus enjoyed a reciprocity. Stars needed hangouts to call their own, and hangouts needed the stars. A successful restaurateur wanted stars to occupy his "A" tables, and stars required tables to occupy.

Not that all of the restaurants where the stars ate were mink-stole and dinner-jacket establishments. Some of the most famous eateries – Tick Tock Tea Room and Schwab's Pharmacy soda fountain – were informal and easy on the wallet. Even in some of the flashier spots, like The Brown Derby, the fare was frankly home-style – from meat loaf to corned beef hash. But in keeping with the town's inclination for folly and extravaganza, theme restaurants with exotic dishes have always been a fixture. For the most part, however, the star-studded restaurants were renowned for their sophisticated gourmet kitchens.

Food has always been an obsession in Hollywood. And, to the outside world there's been no end to the fascination of what so-and-so had for breakfast or lunch, be it Jimmy Durante's reported diet of corn flakes and cigars, or Ann Sothern's preference for scattering buttered popcorn instead of croutons on her consomme.

Since Hollywood types are trend conscious — and trend setting — to the nth degree, they usually expected their restaurants to offer the newest and latest in culinary style. In the forties and fifties, as stars traveled between continents, restaurants often strived to reproduce what was being served in Europe's most sophisticated restaurants. In the seventies and eighties, the dawn of nouvelle cuisine, Hollywood chefs focused on serving inventive and more health-conscious fare.

Filmland preferences for restaurants change with the wind, and always have. "Movie people are whimsical," reported *Today's Woman* magazine in 1948. "They swoop unpredictably when they discover a new place and then change their minds and scatter." While new in-spots are born every year, only a scant number of Hollywood haunts have become legends. Even fewer of those legends exist today. Like the movies of their eras, they defined a special slice of American culture. Although these beloved eateries relied upon a sense of style that was particular to the times, their recipes live on, an enduring legacy of Hollywood history.

❧ ❧ ❧

Desi Arnaz and Lucille Ball

The Cocoanut Grove

1921-1989

The Cocoanut Grove epitomized the symbiotic relationship restaurants enjoyed with the picture colony – each enhanced the other's reputation and basked in the other's glow.

The fancy-dress Cocoanut Grove emerged on Wilshire Boulevard at an auspicious time. In the twenties, Hollywood stars were beginning to define glamour for the world, and press agents were eager to help out. The Cocoanut Grove, which looked as grand as any Ziegfeld stage (indeed, its key components were taken from a Valentino movie set), provided the ideal backdrop and photo op. Those photographs telegraphed to fans around the world the news of who was walking on whose arm after a long day at the studio, as well as displaying the *soigné* finery everyone wore.

In the late thirties and forties, live radio broadcasts of the big band music of Freddy Martin ("Mr. Cocoanut Grove") and vocalist Merv Griffin (who many years later would become owner of the Beverly Hilton Hotel, a few miles west on Wilshire Boulevard), Guy Lombardo, Phil Harris, Ozzie Nelson and Rudy Vallee spread the room's fame coast to coast.

Cocoanut Grove

It was also the site of the Academy Awards presentation banquets from 1930 to 1936. The following year, the awards ceremony was moved to Grauman's Chinese Theater – minus dinner.

The Cocoanut Grove opened in the Ambassador Hotel on April 21, 1921, four months after the lodging opened for business. The Ambassador was a deluxe resort complete with bridal paths and stables, a bowling alley, miniature golf course, Olympic-sized swimming pool, even a post office and furrier. Pola Negri, Norma Talmadge, Gloria Swanson, John Barrymore, Scott and Zelda Fitzgerald and Wilson Mizner, who cofounded the original Brown Derby (see "Brown Derby" on page 18) across the street, were among the notables in residence.

Initially, the Ambassador had featured a small nightclub, the Zinnia Grill. It was so popular that management converted the hotel's ballroom into a bigger, better 1,000-seat club. For decor, artificial palm trees were recycled from the set of Rudolph Valentino's *The Sheik*. To be sure, plenty of papier mâché coconuts hung from treetops along with artificial monkeys with electrically lighted eyes. Stars twinkled overhead and hundreds of little lamps flickered on tables positioned around the dance floor. A grand staircase expressly tailored for grand entrances led to it all.

The Cocoanut Grove quickly become an important meeting place – especially on Tuesday nights – for Hollywood royalty such as Charlie Chaplin, Carole Lombard, Claudette Colbert, Lionel Barrymore, James Cagney, Jack Benny and Dorothy Lamour, while performing on stage were the country's biggest stars such as Fanny Brice, W.C. Fields, Eddie Cantor, and later, Nat King Cole, Tony Martin, Judy Garland, Eddie Fisher and Lena Horne.

Romances were ignited here – including that of Jack Benny and Mary Livingston, whose first date was under

California Oysters St. James

18 California oysters
St. James Butter (recipe below)
Parmesan cheese

Open the oysters on the half shell. Set them in a baking dish, covering each completely with St. James Butter. Sprinkle with Parmesan cheese. Bake until browned and serve very hot. Serves 3.

St. James Butter

1 clove garlic, minced
1 tablespoon chopped chives
1 tablespoon shallots
dash paprika
pinch of parsley
1 drop Tabasco sauce
½ green pepper, diced
¼ pound salted butter at room temperature

Combine garlic, chives, shallots, paprika, parsley, Tabasco and pepper. Blend into softened butter.

the coconuts. Here, also, careers were regularly launched. As chronicled in Margaret Tante Burk's *Are the Stars Out Tonight? The Story of the Famous Ambassador and Cocoanut Grove*, Mack Sennett discovered Bing Crosby performing on stage, and Joan Crawford (*neè* Lucille Le Sueur) frequently bagged trophies in the club's regular dance contests.

The hotel's French chef, Henri, was inspired by a bounty of local produce and fish to create an early version of French-California cuisine. He designed dishes highlighting oranges, avocados, grapefruit and asparagus, as well as local abalone, sand dabs and tiny Cali-fornia oysters, which were served both raw and cooked. One of his most popular dessert concoctions utilized the ubiquitous southern California fig.

In the fifties, the room was modernized, but throughout the decade and into the sixties, the club was losing its luster. Tastes in entertainment changed, and the mid-Wilshire area was no longer stylish or convenient for people living on the Malibu/Beverly Hills axis. For history's sake, the Ambassador will be remembered as much for its past glamour as for tragedy. On June 5, 1968, Robert F. Kennedy was assassinated in the Ambassador's Embassy Room during his California

Raw Oysters with Cocktail Sauce

1 pint commercial chili sauce
1 pint catsup
3 tablespoons fresh horseradish
¼ cup each red and green peppers, chopped
¼ cup blanched celery, chopped
lemon juice
salt
100 raw oysters
Tabasco sauce

Combine chili sauce, catsup, horseradish, peppers and celery. Season with lemon juice, salt and Tabasco sauce. Makes one quart. Spoon 2 or 3 teaspoons onto each oyster. Serves about 25.

presidential primary victory celebration.

The Cocoanut Grove was reinvented in 1970 with the help of Sammy Davis Jr., who arrived by motorcycle to launch the "Now Grove" with glitzy, Las Vegas-style acts such as Sonny and Cher and Diana Ross. But in 1989, the venue and the hotel closed for good. A group of investors including Donald Trump bought the hotel and acreage, and the Los Angeles school board looked into plans to demolish the historic building and construct a high school on the grounds. As of this writing, the building still stands. Also living on are the memories of some of the sophisticated dishes and cocktails concocted inside.

California Figs Romanoff

1 dozen ripe figs, cut in quarters
curaçao, to taste
1 quart vanilla ice cream, very soft
1 pint whipped cream
dash nutmeg

Place figs in a serving bowl. Add a slight flavoring of curaçao to taste. In another bowl, thoroughly mix vanilla ice cream with well-sweetened whipped cream. Pour over figs. Sprinkle with nutmeg and refrigerate. Serve very cold. Serves 6. (Strawberries can be substituted, but omit nutmeg.)

Cocoanut Grove Cocktail

2 ounces dry gin
½ ounce maraschino liqueur
dash of lime juice
dash of grenadine

Shake ingredients into cracked ice, strain and serve.

❧ ❧ ❧

Gracie Allen and George Burns

The Brown Derby

1926-1985

Angelenos have always had a fondness for whimsical architecture, including fast-food stands shaped like hot dogs and drive-through-the-donut snack shops. The original Brown Derby, a restaurant shaped like a hat, was the most famous and chimerical of them all. And it was certainly the most eye-catching place to emerge on Wilshire Boulevard in the twenties. Located across the street from the Ambassador Hotel, The Derby lured diners with a sign perched on top of the crown urging them to "Eat in the Hat."

Many versions of just how and why a derby was chosen have been passed down through the years. One account argues that the hat was chosen as a classy symbol for the newly moneyed and sophisticated folk of Hollywood; another, that co-founder Wilson Mizner fancied the hat worn by Al Smith, the governor of New York, during a visit to Los Angeles. Or perhaps Mizner liked it because it was the garniture favored by gambler Bat Masterson.

In any case, the droll-looking eatery was an instant hit in 1926 for owners Herbert Somborn, an entrepreneur and ex-husband of Gloria Swanson, and Mizner, a well-known wit and writer. Studio head Jack Warner supposedly put up the

cash as the silent partner. With its circular counter, derby-domed lighting fixtures and waitresses wearing starched, derby-shaped skirts, there was absolutely nothing else like it around. It appealed to celebrities such as Charlie Chaplin, W.C. Fields, John Barrymore and Sid Grauman because the food was good – plus the place stayed open until 4 a.m.

Three years later, a second Derby made its debut at the intersection of Hollywood Boulevard and Vine Street, a location which The Derby helped immortalize. This location, minus the derby architecture, was even more packed with stars since it was situated so close to many movie studios. It was not uncommon to find various actors and actresses dropping in for lunch in full makeup and costume.

At one point, during Hollywood's – and The Derby's – Golden Age, the Vine Street location stayed open 24 hours a day, seven days a week. The most prominent customers – Katharine Hepburn, Joan Bennett, Jean Harlow, William Powell and Joan Crawford – sat in booths on the desirable north side beneath caricatures of themselves drawn originally by artist Eddie Vitch, who sketched in exchange for meals. It was here that the peculiarly Hollywood-style practice of paging patrons and delivering telephones to their tables started.

Besides feeding filmmakers, The Derby was featured in 27 films. In *What Price Hollywood?*, Constance Bennett plays a waitress who is discovered while working at the original Derby. Buoyed by the work of an enterprising press agent, the restaurants' fame spread even further. In the glory days of Hollywood in the thirties and forties, two other Derbys were built, in Beverly Hills and Los Feliz.

Robert H. Cobb took over as owner after Somborn's death in 1934 and became the namesake of the now-generic chopped salad so popular with Hollywood

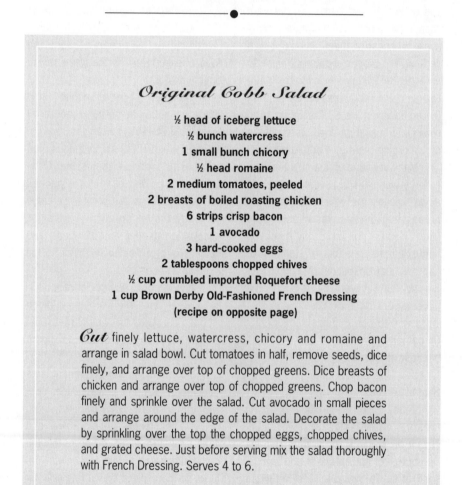

Original Cobb Salad

½ head of iceberg lettuce
½ bunch watercress
1 small bunch chicory
½ head romaine
2 medium tomatoes, peeled
2 breasts of boiled roasting chicken
6 strips crisp bacon
1 avocado
3 hard-cooked eggs
2 tablespoons chopped chives
½ cup crumbled imported Roquefort cheese
1 cup Brown Derby Old-Fashioned French Dressing
(recipe on opposite page)

Cut finely lettuce, watercress, chicory and romaine and arrange in salad bowl. Cut tomatoes in half, remove seeds, dice finely, and arrange over top of chopped greens. Dice breasts of chicken and arrange over top of chopped greens. Chop bacon finely and sprinkle over the salad. Cut avocado in small pieces and arrange around the edge of the salad. Decorate the salad by sprinkling over the top the chopped eggs, chopped chives, and grated cheese. Just before serving mix the salad thoroughly with French Dressing. Serves 4 to 6.

stars who were continually watching their waistlines. Equally popular at lunchtime, however, was the more caloric corned beef hash. Afterwards, many customers couldn't resist finishing off a meal with a slice of the famous Grapefruit Cake.

Although The Brown Derby restaurants are now closed, they live on through a licensing corporation. The company and trade name were bought by Walter Scharfe and Elizabeth Khittle-Scharfe, who held on to the entire contents of the Vine Street Derby after it closed in 1985. Today The Derby is remembered at Walt Disney and MGM Studios Tours in Orlando, Florida, where the Original Cobb Salad and Grapefruit Cake are still served. At this writing, a Derby featuring an exact replica of the Vine Street interior – original black leather booths, chandeliers, caricatures and all – is scheduled to open in Glendale, California. As for the original hat, the outcry of architectural preservationists spared it from the wrecker's ball. Today, however, the hat sits ignominiously on the top of the second story of a mini-mall erected on the corner of Wilshire and Alexandria, site of the original Hollywood haunt.

Brown Derby Old-Fashioned French Dressing

1 cup water
1 cup red wine vinegar
1 teaspoon sugar
juice of ½ lemon
2½ teaspoons salt
1 teaspoon ground black pepper
1 tablespoon Worcestershire sauce
1 teaspoon English mustard
1 clove garlic, chopped
1 cup olive oil
3 cups salad (vegetable) oil

Blend together all ingredients except oils. Then add olive and salad oils and mix well again. Chill. Shake before serving. Makes about 1½ quarts. This dressing keeps well in the refrigerator. Can be made and stored in a 2-quart Mason jar.

Pan-Fried Corned Beef Hash

1 pound lean, extra well-done corned beef brisket
1 cup diced boiled potatoes
1 tablespoon slightly browned onions, chopped fine (optional)
dash of pepper
butter
two eggs (optional)

Grind or chop corned beef very fine. Place in mixing bowl, add potatoes, onions if desired, pepper, and mix well. Should mixture be too dry add a small amount of cold water. Mold into 6-ounce patties and brown in butter on both sides. At the Brown Derby, the dish was served with a poached egg on top. If it is not practical to use fresh corned beef, a 1-pound can of corned beef can be substituted. Serves 2.

Grapefruit Cake

1½ cups sifted cake flour
¾ cups sugar
1½ teaspoons baking powder
½ teaspoon salt
¼ cup water
¼ cup vegetable oil
3 eggs, separated
3 tablespoons grapefruit juice
½ teaspoon grated lemon rind
¼ teaspoon cream of tartar

Sift together flour, sugar, baking powder and salt into mixing bowl. Make a well in center of dry ingredients. Add water, oil, egg yolks, grapefruit juice and lemon rind. Beat until very smooth. Beat egg whites with cream of tartar separately until whites are stiff but not dry. Gradually pour egg yolk mixture over whites, folding gently with a rubber spatula until just blended. Do not stir mixture. Pour into an ungreased 9-inch springform pan. Bake at 350 degrees for 25 to 30 minutes, or until cake springs back when touched lightly with finger. Invert on cake rack and cool. Run spatula around edge of cake. Carefully remove from pan. With serrated knife, gently cut layer in half.

———•———

Grapefruit Cream Cheese Frosting

2 6-ounce packages cream cheese
2 teaspoons lemon juice
1 teaspoon grated lemon rind
¾ cup powdered sugar, sifted
6 to 8 drops yellow food coloring
1 1-pound can grapefruit sections, well-drained

Let cream cheese soften at room temperature. Beat cheese until fluffy. Add lemon juice and rind. Gradually blend in sugar. Beat until blended. Add coloring. Crush several grapefruit sections to measure 2 teaspoons. Blend into frosting. Spread frosting on bottom half of cake. Top with several grapefruit sections. Cover with second layer. Frost top and sides, garnish with remaining grapefruit sections.

✿ Bullock's Wilshire Tea Room ✿

1929-1993

Located atop one of the city's most elegant and beloved department stores, the Bullock's Wilshire Tea Room was one of Los Angeles' longest-running hits. By the time it and the store closed on April 2, 1993, the Tea Room was a dowager of 63½ years. Longtime patrons were teary-eyed, if not outraged, when it was announced that the store's restaurant would close. During its frantic last days, people lined up for hours to eat their last lunch and take one last look. For the first time in years, the garden-style room papered with cabbage roses and framed with trellises was filled to capacity.

A dazzling Moderne tower, Bullock's Wilshire opened for business on then-tony, suburban Wilshire Boulevard on September 26, 1929, one month before the stock market crash.

Located just a short drive east from the Brown Derby, nothing around matched the luxury inside, from its marble-lined walls to its glorious murals and seven Sonia Delaunay carpets.

The store served L.A.'s burgeoning "carriage trade," including wealthy professionals and newly moneyed stars such as Greta Garbo, Marlene Dietrich, Mae West, Joan Crawford, Katharine Hepburn, Ingrid Bergman, Bob Hope, Ray Milland and Jackie Cooper. Angela Lansbury worked as a main floor cashier, and June Lockhart worked in the Collegian department. Former First Lady Pat Nixon also toiled in the Art Deco shrine to shopping.

Founders John Bullock and P.G. Winnett saw to it that Bullock's Wilshire was the ultimate shopping experience. You could buy a wedding gown or a mink stole, a riding habit or a made-to-measure tuxedo. During World War II, Clark Gable and Carole Lombard, dedicated Bullock's-Wilshire shoppers and Tea Room goers, even had his-and-her ski suits made there.

On the fifth floor, there was sustenance to revive a shopper's lagging energy. The dining areas originally included a Tea Lounge, Club Room, two private dining rooms, one semi-private dining room and Tea Patio. By the late forties, the area was modified into the Tea Room and remained in place for 40-plus years. From opening day, fluffy coconut cream pie, baked daily, was a teatime specialty. At lunch, women shoppers favored sandwiches and dainty fare, including the Bombay salad.

Over the years, fashion designers from Pierre Balmain to Gianni Versace and Donna Karan, and stars such as Meryl Streep and Whoopi Goldberg could be spotted in the Tea Room. In 1988, the store held a lunch in honor of the Duke and Duchess of York, Andrew and Sarah, in the East Tea Room.

Coconut Cream Pie

FILLING

3 cups half and half
½ cup sugar
¼ cup egg yolks (approximately 6 yolks)
1 tablespoon corn starch
1 tablespoon butter
¼ teaspoon vanilla extract
⅛ teaspoon almond extract
1 tablespoon Coco Lopez canned cream of coconut (or coconut syrup)

●

CRUST

1 cup flour
⅓ cup shortening
⅛ teaspoon salt
⅛ cup cold water

●

TOPPING

2 cups heavy cream
½ cup sugar
1 teaspoon vanilla extract
coconut flakes

To make filling, cook half and half and sugar in double boiler for two hours. In a mixing bowl, beat together egg yolks, corn starch and butter. Add the vanilla, almond extract and coconut syrup to the mixture and set aside. When the half and half has comes to a boil, add yolk mixture, folding in gently. Set aside to cool for about 1 hour.

To make crust, mix ingredients together in a bowl. Roll out in a circle. Shape into a pie tin. Bake at 250 degrees for 20 minutes on top shelf of oven. Let cool.

To make topping, whip together cream, sugar and vanilla extract.

Fill pie crust with filling, then cover with topping. Sprinkle with coconut flakes.

During the run, *maitre d'* Humberto Lara became an institution. Pompadoured and polite, the dark-suited man was the Tea Room's ultimate greeter and hand-kisser for more than 30 years.

In 1988, Bullock's Wilshire merged with I. Magnin and was renamed I. Magnin Bullocks Wilshire, the Landmark Store. But the neighborhood had lost its luster. In the spring 1992 riots, the store was a target, suffering some $10 million in damages. Even after repairs were made, customers were still reluctant to return. On April 2, 1993, the store closed in the midst of increased demand for discount shopping.

Bombay Salad

5 ounces bay shrimp
5 ounces crab, pieces or shredded
5 ounces thinly sliced celery
½ ounce chopped parsley
1 tablespoon mayonnaise
1 teaspoon soy sauce
shredded lettuce
poppy seed dressing (recipe below)
2 lemon slices

Mix the first six ingredients together. Scoop mixture on lettuce with dressing on the side. Garnish with lemon slice. Serves two.

Poppy Seed Dressing

1 cup sugar
½ cup white vinegar
½ teaspoon ground mustard
3 or 4 drops red food coloring
½ teaspoon salt
1 cup salad oil (not olive oil)
1¼ tablespoons poppy seeds

Blend together all the ingredients except the oil and poppy seeds. Gradually beat in the oil, and when it is well blended, add poppy seeds. Makes approximately 2½ cups.

Tick Tock

Sticky Orange Rolls

1 (2¼-cup) biscuit mix recipe
½ cup plus 2 tablespoons sugar
1 teaspoon grated orange zest
1 teaspoon ground cinnamon
⅛ teaspoon ground cloves
1 (6-ounce) can frozen orange juice concentrate
¼ cup butter

Prepare biscuit dough according to directions. Roll mixture into a rectangle approximately ¼-inch thick. In a bowl, combine 2 tablespoons sugar, orange zest, cinnamon and cloves. Spread the mixture evenly across the dough. Roll dough jellyroll-style and slice into 9 evenly sized pieces.

Meanwhile, heat undiluted orange juice concentrate, butter and ½ cup sugar and stir until completely blended. Pour juice mixture into 8-inch square or round baking dish. Place sliced dough rolls, cut sides down, across juice mixture. Bake at 425 degrees for 20 minutes or until lightly browned. Serve while hot. Makes 9 rolls.

🍂 Tick Tock Tea Room 🍂

1930-1988

Although it didn't sparkle with the glow of bugle-beaded gowns shimmering in candlelight or witness a parade of chauffeured Rolls-Royces at its welcome mat, the Tick Tock Tea Room earned a special standing in early Hollywood.

Even without glitter, the Tick Tock, located at 1716 N. Cahuenga in the heart of downtown Hollywood, was a well-liked restaurant known for serving heaping portions of comfort food to the aspiring actors and studio craftspeople who couldn't afford to dine in the city's tonier restaurants. Stars? While only Francis X. Bushman would admit to frequenting the humble Tick Tock, everyone did.

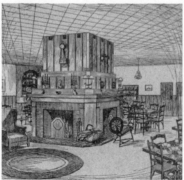

In the thirties and forties, the restaurant was popular for its three-course dinners; in those days the Tick Tock served 2,000 customers a day. And if a regular didn't make an appearance for a while, one of the owners would place a call just to see if he or she were okay.

Norwegian immigrant Arthur Johnson and his wife Helen opened for business in 1930 and installed an old clock, a family treasure, on the wall – hence the quaint epithet. More clocks followed. The final tally of antique timepieces was 48, plus a neon clock as a sign out front.

Once you placed your dinner order – only complete dinners were available – a basket of beloved Sticky Orange Rolls, sweet enough to be dessert, would arrive. The meal began with two appetizers such as canned fruit cocktail or a glass of tomato juice, followed by a paper cup full of sherbet. Next were the entrees – such all-American tasties as meat loaf, fried chicken with gravy, roast pork and applesauce, or fried beef liver and onions. Then came dessert – some kind of homemade pie or cake.

By the eighties, the Tick Tock had become a landmark by virtue of its ability to merely survive in a fast-food world. During that decade, you could find Paul "Pee-wee Herman" Reubens eating there. But, in 1988, eight years after Johnson's death, the restaurant closed.

Mama Weiss

❧ Mama Weiss' Restaurant ❧

1930-1954

Back when Rodeo Drive was home to bungalow courts and you could still ride horses down Sunset Boulevard, the Depression made a culinary heroine out of a warm, jolly and rotund Hungarian immigrant who transformed her family's front bungalow apartment into Mama Weiss' Restaurant.

Bank failures in 1929 had forced the closing of Joseph Weiss' Fine Furniture, Upholstery and Decorating, which had manufactured furniture for Pickfair, Mary Pickford and Douglas Fairbanks' grand English Tudoresque estate. When that happened, his wife Francesca decided to find a way to support the family.

At first, she went to work as a cook for S.N. Behrman, a leading Broadway playwright turned Hollywood screenwriter. But in 1930, Behrman moved back to New York, so Mama decided to turn the Weiss family living and dining rooms on Rodeo into a small, truly home-style restaurant. (In later years, "Prince" Michael Romanoff razed that same bungalow and built his own restaurant on the site (see "Romanoff's" on page 52).

Six months into Weiss' new venture, silent-screen star Mary Miles Minter (reportedly a suspect in the unsolved 1922 murder of director William Desmond Taylor) put up the money to enable Mama to move the family's lodging and restaurant into a larger, two-story house across the street at 309 N. Rodeo, where Mama Weiss' remained for 18 years. In 1947, the restaurant moved to another location on South Beverly Drive.

From the beginning, Mama had no trouble finding customers for the homey atmosphere and predominately Hungarian and Austrian menu she prepared. They loved the blintzes, strudel, goulash, stuffed cabbage, *Wiener schnitzel*, paprika chicken, and the cheese noodle casserole. Some Jewish dishes also hit the spot. Chicken Abe Lastfogel – matzo-ball soup with carrots, chicken and noodles – was named for a top Hollywood agent (and later president and chairman of the William Morris Agency) who, with his wife, Frances, ordered the dish every Friday night.

Among the patrons were actors Edward G. Robinson, Jack Benny, Charles Laughton and his wife, Elsa Lanchester, Johnny Weissmuller and his mate, Lupe Velez; Behrman and all his literary pals; and members of Hollywood's European refugee community, such as directors Ernst Lubitsch and Billy Wilder and actress Luise Rainer.

After a long night in the kitchen, Mama loved to step into the dining room in her gingham dress and white apron and sing Hungarian lullabies, German *lieder* and Viennese operetta, accompanied by a Gypsy violinist. In her prime, she was also the star of her own television cooking program, *The Mama Weiss Show*, which aired six days a week on KHJ in the fifties. Mama finally retired in 1954.

Today, her son, Milton, daughter-in-law Kathie, and granddaughter, Andrea, carry on Mama's family tradition at The Players (no relation to Preston Sturges' Players), a restaurant which opened in 1992 on Little Santa Monica Boulevard just a few paces from Rodeo Drive. The menu is primarily contemporary California-style, but The Players still serves Mama's paprika chicken, one of the most famous of all Hungarian dishes.

Paprika Chicken

2 medium onions, diced
2 tablespoons shortening
2½ pounds chicken parts
1 teaspoon paprika
salt
pepper
2 tablespoons flour
½ pint sour cream
½ cup water or chicken stock

Sauté the onions in the shortening. Add paprika, salt and pepper, to taste. Add the chicken pieces and cover pot. Let it cook on a moderate flame in its own juice for about 30 minutes or until tender. Blend the flour and sour cream and add it to the pot. Add ½ cup water or chicken stock and cook for a few more minutes. Serves 3 to 4.

Cheese Noodle Casserole

1 pound hoop cheese
1 pound flour
7 eggs
6 tablespoons melted butter or margarine
5 tablespoons sugar
5 tablespoons sour cream
the rind of ½ lemon, grated
½ cup white raisins
1 tablespoon powdered sugar
2 teaspoons lemon juice
bread crumbs

Knead the cheese, flour and 3 eggs into a dough. Roll dough thin and cut into 1" wide noodles. Boil for 5 minutes. Strain and run cold water over noodles. Pour melted butter over noodles.

Separate 4 eggs. Add 5 tablespoons sugar, sour cream, lemon rind and raisins to the yolks and mix. Beat 4 egg whites until stiff, adding 1 tablespoon powdered sugar and 2 teaspoons lemon juice as you beat. Fold egg whites into the yolk mixture and add the noodles.

Coat a casserole dish with melted butter and sprinkle it with bread crumbs. Add noodle mixture and bake for 20 minutes at 375 degrees.

Perino's

1932-1985

The swells dined at Perino's – not just movie stars, but dignitaries, U.S. presidents and stalwarts of Los Angeles society. For five decades, it was deemed one of Los Angeles' most elegant restaurants. The courtly Alexander Perino once calculated that he trained the owners of at least 18 restaurants in town.

Chasen's may have been clubbier, the kind of place where movie types ate hobo steak and chili and communed among themselves. But at Perino's, you wore your best jewelry, flashed a gold cigarette case and nibbled on salmon in aspic, breast of pheasant and tangerine soufflé. In the thirties, movie fans kept vigil outside Perino's to catch a glimpse of drop-dead glamorous stars such as Gloria Swanson, Greta Garbo and Cole Porter alighting from their cars.

The youngest of 12 children of a wine merchant from a small town near Lake Maggiore in Italy, Perino longed to become a blacksmith, but his family sent him to apprentice in a pastry shop instead. At 15, he arrived in New York to work as a potwasher in one restaurant and as a busboy at the Plaza Hotel. After working his way up to captain and then

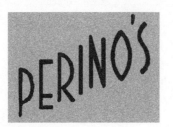

maitre d', he shifted coasts in 1925. Following a stint as a waiter at Los Angeles' Biltmore Hotel downtown, he became head waiter at Victor Hugo's in Beverly Hills, then considered the finest restaurant in the city. Perino, though, decided he could run a better place and opened his eponymous restaurant in 1932.

Not only was food critical to Perino, but so were service and setting. He imported 24-inch-square woven linen napkins from Ireland and employed one waiter for every eight diners, plus two helpers just to polish the silver. He hired architect-to-the-stars Paul R. Williams, who had previously built the MCA agency building and Saks Fifth Avenue department store in Beverly Hills, to design his pink-toned restaurant with an oval dining room at 4101 Wilshire Boulevard. (The first location at 3927 Wilshire – previously the site of Herbert Somborn's failed attempt at an upscale Brown Derby called Hi-Hat – burned to the ground in 1955.)

More than anything, Perino abhorred shortcuts in the kitchen. He insisted, for example, on homemade brown stock and fresh tomato puree for basic spaghetti Bolognese sauce. (Garlic was verboten, though – Perino couldn't stand it.) For salads, he used wine vinegar made from the first pressing of grapes. Refrigerating tomatoes, he believed, destroyed their flavor.

Although the menu changed daily, it always included some classic authentic Italian fare – polenta, canneloni, ravioli, gnocchi – as well as fresh fish such as dover sole, sand dabs and whitefish used in the Whitefish Italienne recipe that follows.

In 1969 Perino sold the business to Esgro Inc., owner of the Chalet Gourmet stores, and, for a short time, he remained as a consultant. The new owner reopened Perino's in a downtown office tower, and supposedly planned to market Perino's Candlelight Dinners in the frozen-food section of grocery stores. Neither venture flew. Yet another buyer of the Wilshire location came to the rescue, but Perino's last gasp was in 1985.

Sauce Italienne

⅓ cup clarified unsalted butter
½ medium onion, diced
4 beefsteak tomatoes, peeled
2 tablespoons tomato paste
¼ teaspoon black pepper
2 teaspoons sugar
1 teaspoon salt
dash nutmeg

In a skillet, heat butter and add onion. Cook until tender but not brown. Cut tomatoes in half horizontally, squeeze out and discard seeds and juice, and dice remaining pulp. Add to the onion along with tomato paste, pepper, sugar, salt and nutmeg. Stir. Simmer 15 minutes. Makes about 2 cups.

Whitefish Italienne

1 (4-pound) whole whitefish, dressed
1 tablespoon unsalted butter
2 teaspoons diced shallots
4 ounces sliced mushroom caps
5 drops lemon juice
salt
½ cup dry white wine
Sauce Italienne (opposite page)
chopped parsley

Fillet the whole fish, trimming off any skin. Clarify butter by melting it over low heat in small saucepan. Do not allow butter to boil. Save clear fat and discard solids.

Heat butter in skillet, adding shallots and fish. Place mushrooms on top of fish. Add lemon juice, salt and wine. Cover the fish with either wax paper or a lid so that steam can escape while it is cooking. Cook slowly over medium heat for about 10 minutes. Remove from heat and transfer fish and mushrooms to warm platter. Reduce pan liquid by half over medium heat, keeping lid or wax paper on skillet to prevent too much steam from escaping. Then add Sauce Italienne to the liquid and cook another 2 to 3 minutes. To serve, pour sauce over fish and garnish with chopped parsley. Boiled potatoes and a green vegetable make a nice accompaniment. Serves 6.

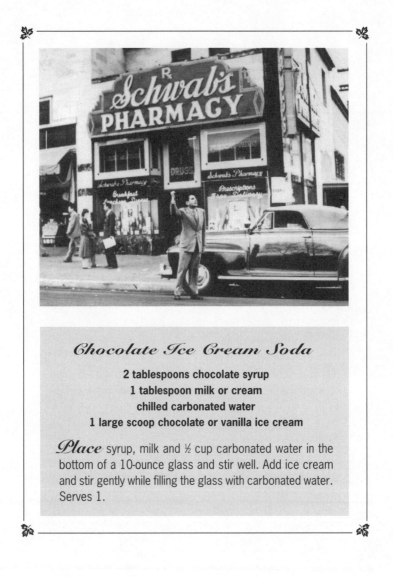

Chocolate Ice Cream Soda

2 tablespoons chocolate syrup
1 tablespoon milk or cream
chilled carbonated water
1 large scoop chocolate or vanilla ice cream

Place syrup, milk and ½ cup carbonated water in the bottom of a 10-ounce glass and stir well. Add ice cream and stir gently while filling the glass with carbonated water. Serves 1.

❧ Schwab's Pharmacy ❧

1935-1988

Popular belief not withstanding, the soda fountain at Schwab's Pharmacy was not the spot where Lana Turner was discovered. It was close, though, geographically, and she *was* a customer. But Hollywood High student Judy Turner was first sighted by Billy Wilkerson, owner of La Rue (see page 56) and publisher of the *Hollywood Reporter*, a few miles away at the Top Hat Soda Shop in 1935.

Still, there is no disputing that the world's most famous drugstore was a landmark on par with the Hollywood sign. So popular with the movie crowd, in fact, was Schwab's that it earned the sobriquet "Schwabadero," in deference to the decidedly more chic Trocadero Club.

Brothers Leon, Bernard, Martin and Jack Schwab, all pharmacists, owned at one time six family drugstores around town. The first was on 6th Street in downtown Los Angeles. In 1935 Leon opened the Hollywood branch located at 8024 Sunset Boulevard, a propitious address at the base of residential Laurel Canyon, on the edge of Sunset Strip and a few paces from the Garden of Allah.

Schwab's was a social leveler. In the thirties and forties, Charlie Chaplin, Harold Lloyd, Ida Lupino, Mickey Rooney, Marilyn Monroe, Judy Garland, Clark Gable, Orson Welles, and the Marx and Ritz Brothers ate eggs and onions, lox and bagels at breakfast, or steaks at dinner, alongside agents, columnists, bit players and nobodies hoping to become somebodies. Ronald Reagan was one of the noted successes who spent time there. Hopefuls like Ava Gardner and Hugh O'Brian worked behind the counter preparing the ice cream sodas.

The Schwabs encouraged patronage from people on all rungs of the ladder of success. Anyone low on money was "comped," as was the case with Lucille Ball in her chorus days. But if you had plenty of dough you could cash a check or have a bottle of aspirin delivered all the way to Malibu if necessary. Prescriptions were filled through the night. A sign near the counter reading, "Coffee 40 cents per cup. Maximum 30 minutes," was largely ignored.

In later years, the waiters and waitresses were mature, understanding types. Cher bought lipsticks by the dozen, and California Governor Jerry Brown and his girlfriend Linda Ronstadt populated the place. And, recalled Leon, *she* paid.

Schwab's closed in 1988, and a super-mall took its place. Like Schwab's itself, the sodas that Andy Hardy and young Americans consumed by the gallons have been eclipsed, but are not forgotten.

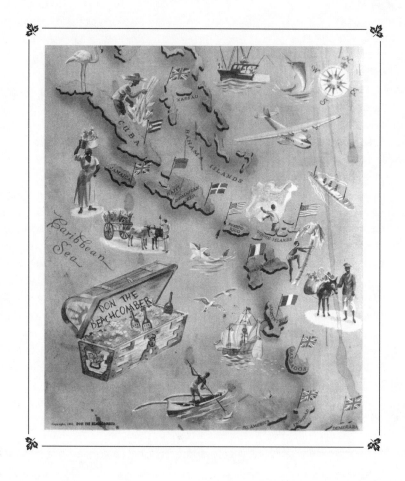

🌿 *Don the Beachcomber* 🌿

1937-1987

The story of Don the Beachcomber began shortly after Prohibition. A small-town Minnesota schoolteacher with a big imagination named Cora Irene Sund saved enough money so that she could move to Los Angeles and secured a job as a waitress at the Tick Tock Tea Room, a family restaurant (see "Tick Tock Tea Room" on page 28). Cora soon met an inventive bartender, Ernest Raymond Beaumont-Gantt, who served exotic rum drinks at his tacky tropical bar located in a Hollywood hotel. His moniker was "Don the Beachcomber." When the schoolteacher and bartender mated, Hollywood's first tropical restaurant was born.

Mildred Pierce had nothing on Cora Irene (a.k.a. "Sunny Sund" and "Mama C.I."), who borrowed money and began to make improvements in the bar, becoming the company's president and Don's wife. By May 1937, she moved Don's restaurant to a more fitting location across the street at 1727 N. McCadden Place. There the couple created their own Hollywood-influenced, romantic notion of a tropical paradise, a real "concept" restaurant, complete with artificial rainstorms designed to romantically pitter patter down on the corrugated iron roof.

Filmland potentates have always had a soft spot for hidden hot spots, and Don the Beachcomber's was just that. From the outside, the place, surrounded in a forest of bamboo, was hard to find, save for a small sign that was intentionally made difficult to read – the underlying message being that if you didn't know where it was, you didn't belong.

But inside, for L.A.'s first South Seas eatery, the schoolteacher and bartender let their collective fantasies run wild. It was twenty years ahead of Disneyland, and Hollywood's royalty, including the Marx Brothers, Franchot Tone, Bing Crosby, Marlene Dietrich and Greer Garson, basked in its folly. The proof was in their chopsticks, which were enshrined in a glass case.

Small dining rooms, which bore names like "The Black Hole of Calcutta" and "The Cannibal Room," were decorated with palm trees, bananas, coconuts, sea shells, shields, shark's jaws, headdresses and carved wooden gods. At one point, the restaurant included a Chinese grocery store, rum shop, gift shop and lei shop. The island-shaped dining tables were made of varnished woods, and more than a few glamorous creatures received proposals of one sort or another in the provocative, candle-illuminated rooms. Certainly helping things along were Don's intoxicating rum drinks: Missionary's Downfall, Vicious Virgin, Cobra's

Fang and the notorious Zombie. Don's rum concoctions were so ingenious they even impressed drinkers like "Trader" Vic Bergeron.

While Don handled the bar part of the business, Cora Irene hired Chinese cooks to create a South Seas-Cantonese hybrid cuisine that was way beyond the chop suey and chow mein found on the menus of most Chinese restaurants of the day. Dishes were made with then-uncommon ingredients like water chestnuts, bamboo shoots, lichee nuts and oyster sauce imported from China. After feasting on Mandarin duck, diners might order "snow cake" for dessert – a mountain of ice covered with pieces of fresh pineapple and candied kumquats. But one of the most popular concoctions was the rumaki appetizer made with water chestnuts and chicken liver wrapped in "sarongs" of bacon, a perfect mate to Don's deliciously lethal rum drinks.

The schoolteacher and the bartender succeeded in business but failed in their relationship. They divorced in 1940, but continued to work together,

opening Beachcombers in Palm Springs and Chicago.

In 1958, Joe Drown, owner of L.A.'s glamorous Bel-Air Hotel, took over the company with businessman David Price and opened more Beach-combers in Marina del Rey, Newport Beach and Waikiki. A decade later, J. Ronald Getty, son of J. Paul, bought the chain. In 1987, the original Beach-comber was demolished. Although all the restaurants eventually faded out of style, the rumaki lives on in tropical restau-rants and catered parties everywhere.

Rumaki

1 pound chicken livers
1 teaspoon anise seed
3 tablespoons brown sugar
1 tablespoon Kitchen Bouquet
2 bay leaves
1½ teaspoons salt
2 pounds sliced bacon
1 12-ounce can water chestnuts
vegetable oil for deep frying

Combine chicken livers with anise seed, brown sugar, Kitchen Bouquet, bay leaves and salt. Boil slowly for 45 minutes. Drain.

Cut in small chunks. Cut water chestnuts into three pieces, each ¼-inch thick. Place a piece of chestnut with one piece of liver and wrap it with one-half strip of bacon. Secure with tooth-pick exposed on either side. Deep-fry in 400-degree vegetable oil until bacon is crispy. Drain and serve. Rumaki can also be baked at 400 degrees for about 20 minutes. Makes about 50 rumaki.

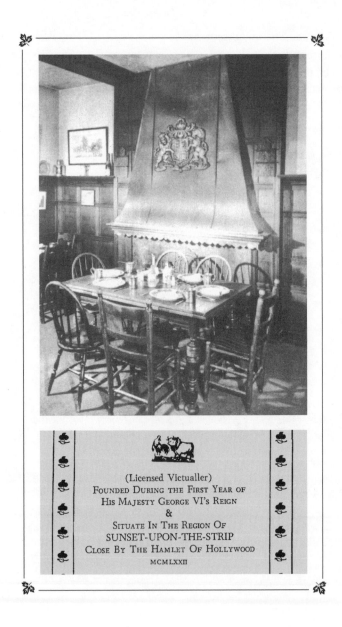

(Licensed Victualler)
FOUNDED DURING THE FIRST YEAR OF
HIS MAJESTY GEORGE VI'S REIGN
&
SITUATE IN THE REGION OF
SUNSET-UPON-THE-STRIP
CLOSE BY THE HAMLET OF HOLLYWOOD
MCMLXXII

Cock 'n Bull

1937-1987

In the twenties and thirties, certain Los Angeles neighborhoods started to resemble movie-studio back lots. Houses, apartment buildings and offices, even the studio edifices themselves, were sprouting up in the shape of Hansel and Gretel cottages, Southern plantations and Tudor manors.

The denizens of filmland particularly took to the English country squire concept, no doubt because so many of them emerged from such pedestrian origins. In 1937, shortly after Hollywood's reigning king and queen, Mary Pickford and Douglas Fairbanks Jr., put the finishing touches on their Tudoresque Pickfair estate in Beverly Hills' Benedict Canyon, the Cock 'n Bull, a small, cozy English pub, opened down the hill at 9170 Sunset Boulevard.

For the next 50 years, the Cock 'n Bull, with its print of Old London over the bar and coat-of-arms stamped china, remained one of the city's most popular watering holes and restaurants.

In the forties, a cocktail invented here called the Moscow Mule became the Cock 'n Bull's signature. "The Drink With a Velvet Kick," as a sign over the bar promised, was a brew of vodka and the establishment's own brand of English ginger beer served in a splendid, iced copper mug. Errol Flynn, F. Scott Fitzgerald, Sinclair Lewis and Somerset Maugham would sit for hours at the bar, which was always populated with an assortment of Hollywood agents and deal makers.

A big American buffet was another attraction, featuring a plethora of turkey and mashed potatoes, and, of course, roast beef and Yorkshire pudding. During World War II, large portions of prime rib were reportedly served and relished here in spite of meat rationing. To start off a meal, many patrons ordered the Welshman's Rabbit, a specialty of the house. It can also be enjoyed as a main course.

Though the most diners preferred their Welshman's Rabbitt served simply with crumpets, the rich cheese delicacy was also served over turkey slices.

This is a Mystery!

Just Imagine This:

Newly-cut Roses stuck in Half a Raw Potato will stay as Sweet-smelling & Beauteous as a Virgin Maid. (Give the humble potato a Sporting Chance to Prove Himself . . . to Her!)

Moscow Mule

1½ ounces vodka
8 ounces ginger beer
juice of ½ lime

Pour vodka into a chilled mug. Add ginger beer to fill mug. Add the lime juice. Decorate mug with a slice of lime.

Welshman's Rabbit

1½ cups milk
1½ pounds aged cheddar cheese, cut into small cubes
4 tablespoons butter
½ cup flour, sifted
2 teaspoons dry hot English mustard
¾ teaspoon cayenne pepper
¼ teaspoon salt
¾ cup beer
2 teaspoons Worcestershire sauce
2 teaspoons A-1 sauce
2 unsparing dashes Tabasco sauce
12 crumpets
6 slices (or more) turkey breast (optional)

Heat milk in double boiler. When warm, add cheese. Stir until well dissolved. In a separate pan, melt butter and add sifted flour, mustard, cayenne pepper and salt. Mix well until a thick paste is formed, then add to milk and cheese, stirring constantly. Cook for 10 minutes. Add beer, Worcestershire sauce, A-1 and Tabasco. Yields 1 quart. Serve over two hot crumpets. As an option, top the crumpets with turkey breast slices and cover with sauce.

Trifle Pudding

¼ pound almond macaroons
¼ pound lady fingers
½ cup raspberry jam
Custard Sauce (recipe below)
¼ cup sherry
¼ cup brandy
maraschino cherries
whipped cream

Use a small glass bowl to hold trifle. Break each macaroon and lady finger in half and mix them together. Spread half of the jam on the inside walls of the bowl. Use about half of the macaroon and lady finger combination to line bowl (cookie mixture will adhere to jam).

Prepare Custard Sauce, adding sherry and brandy. Blend with remaining cookie mixture and pour into lined bowl. Dot the remaining jam on top and refrigerate overnight. Decorate with cherries and whipped cream.

———●———

Custard Sauce

2 cups milk
2 tablespoons cornstarch
3 tablespoons sugar
3 egg yolks
3 tablespoons water

Heat milk in double boiler and stir in cornstarch. Beat together sugar, yolks and water. Add to the hot milk. Stir constantly while cooking for 5 to 10 minutes, until the mixture reaches a thin custard consistency.

Orson Welles with Preston Sturges

The Players

1940-1953

When Preston Sturges wasn't writing and directing some of the wittiest movies ever to emanate from Hollywood —*The Great McGinty, The Lady Eve, Sullivan's Travels* and *The Miracle of Morgan's Creek* among them – he could usually be found inside The Players, both his personal playroom and his Achilles heel for 13 years.

Sturges, who liked to work and eat late, wanted a place to go that was open whenever he or his friends were hungry. In 1938, while under contract to Paramount, he bankrolled Snyder's, a short-lived restaurant run by Ted Snyder, a music publisher who had taught Sturges to write lyrics when he was just getting his start in New York.

When Snyder's failed to catch on, Sturges closed it down and tried to sell off the kitchen supplies and equipment he now owned. Unable to recoup his losses by more than a few cents on the dollar, he decided to open a restaurant himself.

Sturges didn't think small. To house The Players, named for the New York theatrical club, he found a two-story house-turned-wedding chapel on the Sunset Strip. If nothing else, it was well situated, across from the Chateau Marmont Hotel and the Spanish court-yard apartment complex known as Garden of Allah, where many illustrious East Coast writers hibernated during their Hollywood sojourns.

Sturges promptly set about transforming the structure into a tri-level entertainment complex with a restaurant on each floor. Through its various costly face-lifts, The Players eventually grew to include a barber shop and a dinner theater *cum* nightclub known as "The Playroom," where Sturges could stage theatrical productions.

Being there was better than a Fred Astaire movie. After the play ended, the room, with the push of a button, was magically transformed: The floor leveled to become a supper club with an orchestra on a revolving stage.

Opened in 1940, The Players was extremely popular from the start, and continued to be throughout the war years. Regulars included Sturges' cronies in the movie business and the biggest stars of the era, such as Humphrey Bogart, Charlie Chaplin, Barbara Stanwyck, Rudy Vallee, Joel McCrea (who starred in two Sturges films) and his wife Frances Dee, as well as fellow director William Wyler, who was a good friend, and novelist and screenwriter William Faulkner. Sturges himself held court there nightly. Inside the dimly lit rooms, he held cast parties for his movies and courted the women in his life, including his acting discovery,

Frances Ramsden, whom he cast in *The Sin of Harold Diddlebock.*

It was there that Sturges also met his fourth wife, Anne Margaret Nagle. She lived right up the hill. On her way home one night, she noticed that the restaurant's electric sign was dangerously emitting sparks and went to warn the owner of the problem. The following year, she married him on The Playroom stage.

Howard Hughes frequently dined at The Players, sometimes alone, sometimes with a starlet, and sometimes with Sturges. During their many dinners, they came up with the idea for California Pictures Corporation, which turned out to be a disastrous collaboration.

At his peak, Sturges was one of the highest paid men in America, but he had no feel for business. As zany and impractical as any of his heroes, he always insisted on treating his pals and continually dreamed up new inventions for his restaurants such as tables that swiveled out for easy access to a booth. His plans for a helicopter pad in the parking lot so whirlybirds could deliver fresh fish fell through only when the neighbors protested.

Sturges liked good food, and he hired several French chefs to cook sophisticated fare such as hot cheese canapé appetizers, turkey croquettes with supreme sauce and *meringues glacés.* The menu also featured an array of mixed cocktails with amusing names, although Sturges himself drank bourbon old fashioneds. One of The Players' bartenders, Dominick Maggie, went on to open Dominick's on Beverly Boulevard, which became another club-

by entertainment industry hangout.

The Players, a bottomless pit for Sturges' earnings, continually recorded losses. His creditors put it up for sale in 1953. The location – 8225 Sunset – later housed other Hollywood gathering places including the Friars Club, Imperial Gardens and Roxbury.

Side Car Cocktail

1 part cognac
1 part lemon juice
1 part Cointreau

Shake with ice, strain into chilled cocktail glass.

Rob Roy Cocktail

¾ ounce sweet vermouth
1½ ounces scotch
1 to 3 dashes Angostura bitters, optional

Stir in mixed glass containing cracked ice. Strain into chilled glass containing a maraschino cherry.

Jack Rose Cocktail

1½ ounces applejack brandy
½ ounce grenadine
juice of ½ lemon

Shake with cracked ice, strain into cocktail glass.

Myrna Loy with the "prince"

Romanoff's

1941-1962

To an industry driven by fantasy and imagery, Romanoff's was a perfect fit. The Beverly Hills restaurant was the namesake and invention of a self-declared prince with a personality big enough to dazzle the town's most important movers and shakers. Competing studio heads Darryl Zanuck and Jack Warner were among those who put up the money for Romanoff's in Beverly Hills, and "Prince" Mike Romanoff became a celebrity.

The fact was, no one cared whether or not Romanoff was Prince Dimitri Romanoff Obolenski or Grand Duke Michael Romanoff or Harry Gerguson, the orphaned son of a Cincinnati tailor, which apparently he was. His ancestry was merely irrelevant.

When he arrived in Hollywood in 1927, the always dapper Prince Romanoff – known for his trademark spats, moustache and walking stick – lived in hotels, borrowed money from his wealthy pals and charmed everyone in sight. He even spoke with a genuine Oxford accent – although it was believed he acquired it working as a servant in the lofty British university. Still, there was always room for Romanoff on a Hollywood polo team because he was the kind of guy the movie crowd loved having around.

In 1931, a member of the Russian guard branded him a fake, and since he had no citizenship papers or passport to dispute the charge, Romanoff disappeared for a decade. In 1941, he resurfaced, opening the first Romanoff's at 326 N. Rodeo Drive. By 1945, *Life* magazine crowned him "the most wonderful liar in 20th-century U.S.," a description that only seemed to further his restaurant's success.

The place was so popular that its only problem was appeasing the celebrities, who all felt deserving of one of five "A" booths across from the bar. As it was, at lunchtime the first booth was always occupied by Humphrey Bogart, the second by William Morris agent Abe Lastfogel, the third by Louis B. Mayer, the fourth by Darryl Zanuck, and the fifth by Harry Cohn.

So in 1951, Romanoff moved to larger quarters down the street at 240 S. Rodeo Drive, where there was a roof garden, ballroom for private parties, a small private dining room and a much larger dining room designed to accommodate 24 equally-desirable booths. It didn't quite work out that way – people only wanted to be seated on the left of the staircase as they entered, and there were only four booths on that side of the room. Unfortunately, if twelve V.I.P.'s showed up – including, say, Clark Gable, Lana Turner, and Cole

Porter – Romanoff was forced to seat someone in Siberia.

The French cuisine was first rate. Specialties included *coulibiac* of salmon, bouillabaisse *Marseillaise* and saddle of lamb presented on a silver wagon. Dessert was high-drama fare such as cherries jubilee, *crêpes suzettes* and the house specialty, individual chocolate soufflés.

Although business at the new location prospered through the late fifties, after that it became increasingly difficult to fill the room. When all the booths weren't booked, the restaurant, which was starkly decorated and brightly lit (with neither flowers nor candlelight to soften it), looked particularly barren.

By then there was increasing competition from newer restaurants in town, and much of Romanoff's clientele was aging into the old guard. For all Romanoff's charm, he could also offend. One lunchtime he made disparaging remarks about Alfred Hitchcock who appeared to be napping after consuming a large meal. Hitchcock, however, heard every word and never returned.

To stimulate reservations, Romanoff introduced black-tie dinner dances on Thursday nights – "maids' night off" in Beverly Hills. But his political associations doomed him. He became ultra Republican in a community of Democrats, and actually began to distribute political literature on the tables. Much of his clientele found his friendship with J. Edgar Hoover and other highly-placed Republicans to be offensive. Compounding this problem was a financial blunder – opening the disastrous Romanoff's on the Rocks restaurant in Palm Springs.

In 1958, Romanoff achieved his goal of becoming a U.S. citizen by an act of Congress signed by President Eisenhower. His restaurant closed on New Year's Eve, 1962. The following day, Billy Wilder called Romanoff's *maitre d'* Kurt Niklas and offered the support of a group of financial backers, including Jack Benny, Jack Warner and Otto Preminger, for his own restaurant. The Bistro on Cañon Drive, which opened the following year as an entertainment industry haunt in its own right, was the first of three Bistro restaurants to be launched by Niklas. Eventually, the Bistro captain and manager, Jimmy Murphy, opened his namesake power eatery, Jimmy's, adjacent to Century City. It was at the Bistro that Niklas continued to serve the beloved and sinfully rich chocolate soufflés. No one should go through life without sampling one, smothered with freshly whipped cream.

Chocolate Soufflé

6 egg yolks
5½ ounces granulated sugar
dash vanilla
5½ ounces all purpose flour
2 cups milk
2 ounces unsweetened chocolate
2 cups egg whites (approximately 12 egg whites)
dash salt
7 ounces sugar

Preheat oven to 375 degrees. Mix egg yolks with 5½ ounces sugar and vanilla. Add flour and stir until it forms a smooth paste. In heavy-bottomed pot, bring milk to a boil. Add the paste-like mixture to the milk. Let boil 2 to 3 minutes before stirring. Then use a wire whisk to mix, and use a wooden spatula to stir until the paste no longer sticks to the sides of the pot.

In a separate pan, melt chocolate. Meanwhile, put the paste in a standing mixer and beat for approximately 10 to 15 minutes. Add melted chocolate and mix well. Place in a large mixing bowl and let cool.

Place the egg whites in a mixing bowl with a dash of salt and whip until they start to form meringue-like peaks. Then gradually add remaining sugar and continue to beat until stiff. Egg whites should not slide if the bowl is tipped. Add one-fourth of the whites to the paste, folding with a rubber spatula. Continue folding remaining egg whites, one-fourth at a time, until well combined. Spoon into buttered and sugared 5 or 6-ounce souffle dishes. Cook for 15 minutes. When done, sprinkle with powdered sugar and serve with whipped cream. Serves 10 to 12.

Peter Lorre, John Garfield, Humphrey Bogart and Lauren Bacall

La Rue

1945-1969

In the fifties there were two reasons to eat at La Rue: the food was considered to be among the city's finest, and you might get a mention in the *Hollywood Reporter*, one of the industry's trade journals.

Hollywood Reporter founder William R. "Billy" Wilkerson, who owned the restaurant, kept vigil there at table No. 1 and freely plugged the stellar goings-on in his paper.

La Rue, said to be Jack Warner's favorite restaurant and a regular destination for Walt Disney, at 8361 Sunset, was just one of Wilkerson's sidelines. At various times starting in the thirties he owned two of The Strip's most acclaimed night spots, the Cafe Trocadero and Ciro's. Needless to say, Wilkerson's outposts did much to establish the blocks of Sunset between Doheny Drive and Crescent Heights as the town's *ne plus ultra* nightclub and restaurant scene.

His foray into restaurants began when he turned some excess office space into Vendome, a fancy food emporium a few blocks from the *Hollywood Reporter's* offices, duly promoted with ads in the *Reporter*. Besides selling delicacies such as Russian caviar and brandied fruits, he served lunch to stars like Joan Crawford, Marlene Dietrich and Mae West.

Expanding his horizons, in 1934, Wilkerson bought the site of the defunct La Bohème and reopened it as Cafe Trocadero for dining and dancing, although being seen there was far more important than any other activity. These were the days when a sighting by a famous director could launch a pretty girl's career – as was the case with Rita Hayworth who was discovered at the Trocadero by director Howard Hawks.

Wilkerson sold the "Troc" in 1938, and opened Ciro's nearby in 1940. Before he sold out in 1946, rival clubs were opening on Sunset such as Mocambo and the Earl Carroll Theatre. In the early forties, Wilkerson opened the elegant La Rue with Bruno Petoletti and chef Orlando Figini, who opened and managed the Italian Pavilion at the 1939 World's Fair in New York. Petoletti was *maitre d'* at the Pavilion and at The Pump Room in Chicago. Figini went on to become the chef at the Waldorf-Astoria and "21" in Manhattan. When he came to Southern California, Figini was a chef at Ciro's and the Arrowhead Hotel, another of Wilkerson's investments. Figini urged Petoletti to join him at the hotel.

The three men joined forces to create the very French La Rue on a visible corner of what is now known as Sunset Plaza. Stars sat in rich gold leather booths, as opposed to the more prosaic red ones found in other establishments. The red-carpeted main dining room was dominated by two huge crystal chandeliers, which were so elaborate that the proprietors had to regularly summon crystal cleaning specialists from San Francisco.

Figini and Petoletti bought Wilkerson's interest in 1950 and the restaurant closed in 1969.

Until then, Figini's tournedos La Rue, with its savory sauce, was one of the in-crowd's favorite dishes. It was the white truffles that made it unique.

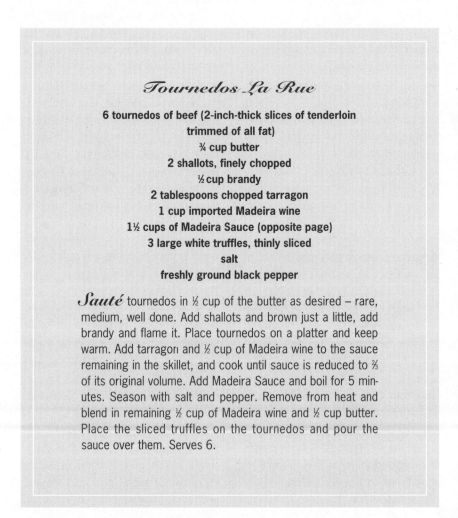

Tournedos La Rue

6 tournedos of beef (2-inch-thick slices of tenderloin
trimmed of all fat)
¾ cup butter
2 shallots, finely chopped
½ cup brandy
2 tablespoons chopped tarragon
1 cup imported Madeira wine
1½ cups of Madeira Sauce (opposite page)
3 large white truffles, thinly sliced
salt
freshly ground black pepper

Sauté tournedos in ½ cup of the butter as desired – rare, medium, well done. Add shallots and brown just a little, add brandy and flame it. Place tournedos on a platter and keep warm. Add tarragon and ½ cup of Madeira wine to the sauce remaining in the skillet, and cook until sauce is reduced to ⅔ of its original volume. Add Madeira Sauce and boil for 5 minutes. Season with salt and pepper. Remove from heat and blend in remaining ½ cup of Madeira wine and ½ cup butter. Place the sliced truffles on the tournedos and pour the sauce over them. Serves 6.

Madeira Sauce

2 tablespoons butter
2 tablespoons flour
2 cups beef bouillon
⅓ cup Madeira wine
salt
freshly ground black pepper

Melt butter over low heat. Add flour and stir until smooth. Add bouillon and cook until thickened, stirring constantly. Stir in Madeira wine, salt and pepper to taste, and simmer for 5 minutes. Makes about 2 cups.

Scandia

1946-1989

*L*ike so many popular restaurants in Los Angeles, Scandia was started by immigrants. After working as a chef at Bit of Sweden, a smorgasbord restaurant on Sunset Boulevard, Kenneth Hansen and his sister, Teddy, natives of Copenhagen, opened Scandia at 9131 Sunset in 1946. Although Teddy was a working co-owner until her death in 1979, Kenneth was always the star and ran the place with an iron fist.

In the early days, he cooked the kind of simple Germanic, brasserie food that was familiar to Hollywood's ethnic population – *kaaldalmer*, or stuffed cabbage, Swedish boiled beef with horseradish sauce, pot roast and brisket. Hungarian-born actor Peter Lorre, who had worked in the theater in Switzerland, Austria and Germany before coming to Hollywood, lunched there every Saturday.

Hansen was a man's man who inaugurated an all-male drinking and eating club called The Vikings of Scandia, whose members were stars and businessmen. Everett Crosby, Bing's brother and manager, was the first Viking chief.

In 1957, the Hansens moved into enlarged quarters across the street at 9040 Sunset. As The Vikings membership grew, stars such as Cornel Wilde, Marilyn Monroe, Gary Cooper, Ingrid Bergman, Marlene Dietrich, Rosalind Russell and Rita Hayworth discovered the restaurant's gracious service and distinctive cuisine.

In the new location, where walls were decorated with coats of arms, the menu began to evolve with more sophisticated Continental and Danish fare, including a salmon appetizer called *gravlaks* (translation: buried). The dish was invented by the Vikings as a way to preserve salmon for the winter by curing it, wrapping it in a sack and burying it in the ground. But the Vikings never knew about Scandia's mustard dill sauce.

As former head chef Hans Prager recalls, new tastes such as *gravlaks and kalvfilet Oscar* – a veal, asparagus and crayfish entree served with bernaise sauce first made for Sweden's King Oscar II at the turn of the century – appealed to Angelenos who were becoming more adventurous in their dining. At the same time, Hansen himself became more sophisticated, traveling back to Scandinavia to bring new recipes to Hollywood.

In its prime, Scandia was considered the finest Scandinavian restaurant in the country, and seafood was flown in year round from the north Atlantic. At Christmas, the Hansens presented authentic holiday foods such as *lutfisk* (lye fish) and roast goose stuffed with apples and prunes.

The Hansens sold Scandia in 1978 to Margie and Robert Petersen, publisher of several magazines including *Teen,* *Hot Rod, Motor Trend* and *Guns & Ammo.* (Mr. Petersen's offices were about a mile away on Sunset and he had eaten lunch at Scandia daily.) Hansen stayed on as a consultant until his death. The restaurant closed in 1989. In 1977, Prager opened The Ritz in Newport, California. As for The Vikings, they still meet monthly for lunch at Jimmy's as a social and philanthropic club.

Gravlaks

1 2-pound piece of salmon, cleaned and boned
3 tablespoons salt
3 tablespoons sugar
1 tablespoon crushed peppercorns
½ bunch dill

Cut salmon in half lengthwise. Place one half, skin-side down, in a baking dish. Sprinkle with half of salt, sugar and peppercorns. Cover with dill. Rub the other half of salmon with remaining salt, sugar and peppercorns and lay this piece over the other (skin side up). Wrap well in foil or plastic. Place weighted plate on top of fish. Refrigerate for 48 hours, turning fish every 12 hours. Each time, unwrap and separate fillets and baste with pan liquid. Then rewrap well. When ready to serve, carefully scrape off dill and seasonings. Place the fish skin-side down on a cutting board and slice very thinly on the diagonal, cutting away from the skin. Serves 24.

If desired, the leftover skin can be cut into narrow strips and fried in deep oil until crisp. Use a piece of crisp skin to garnish each serving.

Mustard Dill Sauce

¼ cup Dijon mustard
3 tablespoons sugar
2 tablespoons vinegar
1 teaspoon dry mustard
⅓ cup oil
3 tablespoons chopped dill

Mix together mustard, sugar, vinegar and dry mustard. Gradually beat in oil until thick, then add dill. Serve cold. Makes ¾ cup.

Pumpernickel Toast

1 loaf pumpernickel bread (unsliced and frozen)
½ cup butter or margarine
1 or 2 cloves crushed garlic
½ cup grated Parmesan cheese

Preheat oven to 275 degrees. Use a sharp knife to slice frozen bread very thinly. Melt butter. Blend in garlic and cheese. Brush one side of bread with butter mixture. Bake in single layers on ungreased baking sheets for about 15 to 20 minutes until crisp. Serve warm. Makes 30 to 40 slices.

CAFÉ

Swiss

Veal Cordon Bleu

12 thin slices veal
freshly ground black pepper
salt
6 thin slices Swiss cheese
6 thin slices boiled Virginia ham
flour
3 eggs, beaten
¾ cup bread crumbs
3 tablespoons butter
1 tablespoon cooking oil
6 lemon slices

Flatten veal with side of a cleaver. Pound on both sides until ¼-inch thick. Sprinkle with salt and pepper. Lay veal slices out flat. Put one slice of cheese and one slice of ham between two veal slices; make six "sandwiches." Pound edges of veal together to seal in filling. Dip each sandwich in flour. Then dip in beaten eggs, finally in bread crumbs. In a large skillet, heat butter and oil. Sauté breaded veal sandwiches over moderately high heat for about 4 minutes on each side or until golden brown. Serve with a lemon slice on top. Serves 6.

Cafe Swiss

1950-1985

Fred Hug, a Swiss-born chef, met and married Laura, a pretty Swiss woman who had studied restaurant management in Switzerland. Although Fred had always dreamt of owning his own little restaurant, acquiring one of the world's most glamorous addresses – 450 N. Rodeo Drive – was probably beyond his wildest ambition at the time.

But Rodeo Drive was still a sleepy neighborhood shopping district in 1950 when the couple took over a small coffee shop and turned it into Beverly Hills' one and only chalet. At lunchtime, it became a sanctuary for stars and executives working at the nearby Twentieth Century-Fox and MGM studios.

Soon after the restaurant opened, the Hollywood crowd – including Clark Gable, Alan Ladd, Gary Cooper, Robert Taylor, Barbara Stanwyck and Jack Benny – gravitated there, especially for lunches on the sunny patio. Gable usually came alone, lunching on a corned beef sandwich and beer and reading the Hollywood trade papers in his favorite corner booth. When Walter Winchell was in town from New York, he frequently dined alone on Saturday nights at the Rodeo Drive eatery.

In later years, Jack Lemmon, Walter Matthau, Natalie Wood and Gene Kelly were among those who dropped in since they lived just a few blocks away.

The Hugs became American citizens in 1955 and hence qualified for a liquor license. Their dimly lit bar became an instant draw. By the sixties it was a mecca for the town's composers, lyricists and arrangers. Joe Marino, who had worked in the music departments at Paramount and MGM, played the piano nightly until 2 a.m., and a Who's Who of his music friends – including Johnny Mercer, Harry Warren, Jimmy Van Heusen, Ned Washington, Jimmy McHugh, Bronislav Kaper, Sammy Fain, Howard Arlen, Conrad Salinger and Sammy Cahn – became habitués.

For more than 30 years until his death, Fred ran "the back," cooking Continental/American cuisine as well as some typical Swiss dishes like veal cordon bleu, a popular dish of the fifties and sixties. Laura – always immaculately turned out in evening gowns and jewels at night – ran "the front" until the Cafe Swiss closed its doors in 1985.

Luau

1954-1978

From the fifties and through out the late seventies, colorful Angelenos remained partial to exotic restaurants, even if their taste buds fancied meat and potatoes.

At the Luau, if you weren't in the mood for Bali Miki (meat on a stick), you could always slice into top-quality steak against a setting of tropical palms, volcanic rock, a lagoon and a rather noisy waterfall. The Polynesian paradise at 427 North Rodeo Drive borrowed Don the Beachcomber's concept, but the special effects were even more extravagant – the men's room even boasted clam-shell urinals.

In addition, co-owner Steve Crane had direct access to the world of show business. He started out as a Hollywood husband, twice, to Lana Turner, whom he met one night at the Mocambo. (His first marriage had not been properly dissolved. Hence a pregnant Turner filed for annulment; they married briefly a second time.)

Crane was a good-looking man-about-town, card player, sometime actor and "charming opportunist," as his and Turner's daughter, Cheryl Crane, explains with Cliff Jahr, in *Detour: A Hollywood Story.* Crane real-

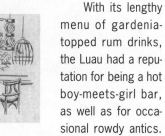

ALOHA

ized he wasn't destined for a big-screen career, but he had an affinity for people and entertaining. In 1946, with his gambling money, he bought Lucy's, an established hangout across the street from Paramount Studios. Eight years later, Crane and his partner, Al Mathes, took over Sugie's Tropics, a Hawaiian restaurant on Rodeo Drive, which they promptly embellished with the lavish Polynesian decor and reopened as the Luau.

There were always plenty of celebrities seated around tables made from lacquered ship hatch covers – from Fred Astaire to the Beach Boys, director Roman Polanski and Sharon Tate, Marlon Brando, Hugh Hefner, John Wayne, Norma Shearer, Lee Marvin, Robert Evans and Candice Bergen. Lana Turner remained Crane's friend and frequent customer.

With its lengthy menu of gardenia-topped rum drinks, the Luau had a reputation for being a hot boy-meets-girl bar, as well as for occasional rowdy antics. Gordon Scott, who starred in several Tarzan movies in the fifties, reportedly was one of many to leap naked into the lagoon.

Crane became one of Los Angeles'

STEVE'S PEARL...

A pearl in every oyster, according to story tellers... who knows? There may be one in this "for ladies only" cocktail...P.S. should be delicately sipped—not gulped.

THE SHARK...

The Shark, not unlike its namesake, is a picture of grace and smoothness. Though small and slender, it is not to be treated lightly.

ZOMBIE...

According to Webster's Unabridged, "the walking dead." Historical Note: This World-famous drink was originated in 1934 by Don "himself" the Beachcomber of Hawaii and Tahiti, and, our own Fong Foo.

biggest restaurateurs before his death in 1985. He created the Kon-Tiki Ports-of-Call restaurants for more than a dozen Sheraton Hotels, and also opened a half dozen other local restaurants, including The Camelot, Scam 9000 and Stefanino's. Nicky Blair – who became Stefanino's co-owner and host – also opened two eponymous Sunset Strip restaurants. In 1977, longtime Luau *maitre d'* Joe Stellini opened Stellini's, another restaurant frequented by the Hollywood community.

In 1979, Rodeo Drive was turning into an international shopping mecca, and the Luau was razed to make way for a lavish, marble-lined shopping complex.

Bali Miki

1 pint catsup
½ cup sugar
1 cup barbecue sauce (any brand)
½ teaspoon finely minced garlic
½ cup white wine
24 6-inch wood skewers
3 pounds beef fillet, cut in small pieces

Stir together catsup, sugar, barbecue sauce, garlic and wine.

Fill wood skewers with pieces of beef. Brush on sauce and broil one minute on each side. Brush on more sauce, and cook a few minutes longer until done. Makes 24 hors d'oeuvres.

Cyrano

1958-1985

The Sunset Strip was swinging in the sixties. You could frug underneath the go-go dancers in gilded cages hanging from the rafters at the Whisky-A-Go-Go, pretend you were a beatnik at Pandora's Box, or listen to barely-known singers like Linda Ronstadt and James Taylor at The Troubadour. And late at night, if you were in the Hollywood groove, you stopped at Cyrano to make the scene over a little French onion soup.

It's no wonder that just as the youth explosion hit, a china shop on The Strip moved out of the neighborhood and a cool new restaurant moved in. In 1958, the year the Dodgers moved from Brooklyn to Los Angeles, Cyrano opened at 8711 Sunset as a coffee-and-sandwich shop. In a short time, Bob Fidler, a young stock trader who had become a millionaire at 15 and had an office across the street, thought he could run a better place and bought it.

Immediately, the town's fresh talents felt comfortable at Cyrano. You didn't need buckets of money to eat here. The place had a party atmosphere, especially late at night. Frequently, if the mood struck, performers such as Joan Rivers and Shecky Greene would entertain. And at a time when L.A.'s serious restaurants still had dress codes requiring jackets and ties for men, at Cyrano you could eat dinner dressed any way you liked – from jeans to bell-bottom tuxedos. "I wanted people to come in their bathing suits," said Fidler.

What a scene! Steve McQueen and his pals would drive up on their motorcycles and slip into the crowd. Producers, directors, production designers and Hollywood's young stars, including Natalie Wood, Robert Wagner, Clint Eastwood, Ben Gazzara, Sal Mineo, Suzanne Pleshette, Bill Cosby and Troy Donahue, showed up, as did the music crowd – Elvis Presley, Neil Diamond, Elton John, Rod Stewart – many of whom lived and worked in the neighborhood. For the stars, the restaurant opened house accounts so that no money would have to leave their hands – bills went directly to business managers' offices. Fidler later became a restaurant consultant and managing partner in Nicky Blair's, another celebrity haunt that opened across the street. He sold Cyrano in 1981. It closed four years later.

But throughout the sixties and into the seventies, Cyrano was a hip late-night hangout. Chef Jacques Laporte had created a menu that was less fussy than the French food at La Rue (see "La Rue" on page 56) up the block. The most popular dishes on the menu, which was a merger of French, Italian and American fare, were lobster tails, spaghetti, and London broil. But it's the old-fashioned French onion soup that Laporte learned from his aunt in Aulus-les-Bain, France, that is recalled with the greatest fondness.

French Onion Soup

2 medium onions, sliced
olive oil
Beef Stock (recipe on opposite page)
6 slices one- or two-day-old French bread
olive oil infused with garlic clove
Parmesan cheese
½ pound provolone or mozzarella cheese

Sauté onions in olive oil until very soft. Add beef stock. Heat until soup boils and then reduce flame to simmer.

Trim bread to the diameter of individual serving crocks. Rub bread with olive oil infused with garlic and sprinkle with parmesan cheese. Bake in hot oven two or three minutes until toasted. Layer one piece of toast over soup-filled crocks and cover with a few slices of provolone or mozzarella cheese. Pop into oven until cheese melts, about two or three minutes. Serves six.

Beef Stock

4 pounds uncooked beef bones cut in 2-inch pieces
2 stalks celery
1 or 2 carrots
1 onion
3 sprigs parsley
1 bay leaf
pinch thyme
3 or 4 garlic cloves
1 medium tomato
salt and pepper

Put all ingredients except herbs, salt and pepper in 500 degree oven and roast one hour to brown. Put everything in a soup pot. Add enough water to cover. Add herbs, salt and pepper. Bring to boil, then reduce flame and simmer slowly for three hours.

To give stock a dark brown color without using artificial coloring, cook one split onion under the broiler until it is brown. Add onion to the stock and continue cooking for another hour. Strain.

Patrick Terrail

Ma Maison

1973-1985

Reverse chic took hold of Hollywood in the early seventies. That's when a brazen Frenchman transformed a carpet warehouse at 8368 Melrose Avenue into a "shower curtain with Astroturf," as owner Patrick Terrail described the most famous patio in town.

Initially Terrail, whose uncle Claude owned the legendary *Tour d'Argent* restaurant in Paris, received poor reviews for his original brochettes-only menu, which he cooked up himself. However within six months he had added an unknown to his staff of chefs – Wolfgang Puck – and Hollywood's most legendary haunt of the seventies took off.

Ma Maison's outdoor dining arrangement was meant to be temporary – Terrail had imagined something more, well, finished when he opened for business in 1973. But the restaurant became successful before Terrail had the chance to decorate. And since this was the era of Gucci loafers and blue jeans, the concept of eating expensive food in a space no finer than a makeshift backyard rumpus room with plastic chairs and four plastic light-up geese made sense for trend-conscious L.A. Anyway, for glitz, all you had to do was count the lineup of Rolls-Royces in the constantly jammed parking lot, and, of course, peek at the beautiful people eating inside.

The best way to describe Ma Maison's drawing power was to list the people who never ate a meal there – Bob Hope and John Wayne. Just about every studio head, actor, agent, manager, United States leader (Nixon, Ford, Kissinger), and Hollywood hopeful made an appearance, usually on a regular basis. Studio financier Kirk Kerkorian and executives Dan Melnick and David Begelman lunched there nearly every day, as did entertainment attorney Greg Bautzer, agent Irving "Swifty" Lazar, and actors David Janssen, Suzanne Pleshette, Jack Lemmon, Roger Moore and Michael Caine. Friday lunches were sacred – unless you had a standing reservation, it was impossible to get a table.

For seven years, until his death, Orson Welles was virtually in residence. He ate lunch and dinner at Ma Maison every day (mostly ordering grilled fish), always sitting at the same table inside because he didn't want to be seen. If, for some reason, the director didn't show, food was sent to his house. When he died, it was Terrail who notified the press.

The success of the laid-back eatery was due initially to well-connected backers – including Gene Kelly, several movie producers and a Hollywood business manager – but also because

Chicken Salad

1 chicken (3 to 3½ pounds)
10 cups Chicken Stock (recipe opposite page) or canned broth
1 red or Golden Delicious apple, peeled, cored and diced
2 celery stalks, peeled and cubed
½ cup fresh mayonnaise (recipe on page 78)
1 tablespoon capers, drained
2 tablespoons grainy mustard
2 tablespoons Dijon mustard
salt and freshly ground pepper to taste
fresh lemon juice to taste
1 head butter or limestone lettuce, washed and dried
¼ cup vinaigrette (recipe on page 78)
2 hard-boiled eggs, halved (garnish)
2 tomatoes, cut in wedges (garnish)
2 bell peppers, sliced (garnish)
8 ounces green beans, blanched (garnish)

Combine chicken and stock in a large pot. Bring to a simmer and cook uncovered for 20 minutes over low heat (never boil). Remove the chicken. When it's cool enough to handle, but still warm, discard skin. Pull meat from the bones and shred by hand into bite-sized pieces. Place pieces in a large mixing bowl.

Add the apple, celery, mayonnaise, capers and mustards to the chicken and combine gently. Taste and adjust seasoning with salt, pepper and lemon juice. Break lettuce into bite-sized pieces and place in another mixing bowl. Toss with vinaigrette. To serve, divide the lettuce among four serving plates. Top each with a serving of chicken salad and garnish as desired. Serve at room temperature. Serves 4.

the food was so good. Terrail – with the now-renowned Puck in the kitchen – offered a revolutionary way of cooking: California-French nouvelle cuisine, emphasizing fresh ingredients on the undercooked side, and all kinds of salads. The menu (illustrated by David Hockney) suited the health-conscious movieland population. At lunchtime, one of the most popular orders was for a low-calorie chicken salad Terrail invented when at New York's L'Etoile. "It was a bad version of a Waldorf," he quipped. Another favorite was the saboyan of fresh fruit with strawberry sauce, concocted by Jean Pierre Lemanissier.

Terrail kept the place running with gall and charm. He never allowed photographers inside and bent over backwards to coddle the clients. (Once Lauren Hutton walked in for lunch carrying a switchblade. She asked Terrail to oil it; he did.) He also created a club-like atmosphere in which former husbands and wives amicably – or maybe not so amicably – dined under the same tent.

One of Terrail's most brilliant public relations moves was not listing the restaurant's phone number, making access to the place all the more desirable. But the unlisted phone number idea was unintentional. Anticipating a flood of tourists after a story that was due to appear in *People* magazine in 1977, Terrail removed the number from the directory and never replaced it.

In 1985, when Ma Maison closed, the *Los Angeles Times* reported that it

---

Chicken Stock

1 pound chicken bones
2 celery stalks, chopped
2 carrots, peeled and chopped
1 onion, chopped
1 bay leaf
10 cups water

Combine all ingredients in a large saucepan and bring to a boil. Skin the foam off the top, reduce to a simmer and cook, uncovered, about two hours. Strain the mixture, discarding the solids, and refrigerate for one hour. When a layer of fat forms at the top, skim and discard. The stock can be stored in a covered container in the refrigerator for 4 to 5 days or frozen indefinitely.

was "the most successful closing in restaurant history," attracting the usual stable of stars, Hollywood wives and the obligatory Rolls-Royces. The finale ensued when competing gourmet hot spots opened, including Wolfgang Puck's Spago. Mark Peel of Campanile, Susan Feniger of City and Claude Segal of Bistango (later Picnic) were all veterans of Terrail's famed kitchen. Puck also went on to open Chinois, Eureka and Granita.

Terrail helped to launch a renewed Ma Maison in an imposing nearby hotel with the designation, Ma Maison Sofitel, but the new restaurant never caught on with the in-crowd, and the dining room shut down except for banquets.

Mayonnaise

2 egg yolks
2 tablespoons fresh lemon juice
1 tablespoon Dijon mustard
1½ cups safflower oil
½ teaspoon salt
⅛ teaspoon white pepper

Combine egg yolks, lemon juice and mustard in a food processor and mix for about 15 seconds. With the machine running, gradually add the oil through the feed tube in a slow, steady stream. When all the oil has been added, add salt and pepper and process briefly to combine. Mayonnaise may be stored in a sealed container in the refrigerator for one week. Don't freeze.

Vinaigrette

1 tablespoon Dijon mustard
¼ cup sherry vinegar
¼ cup extra virgin olive oil
½ cup safflower oil
salt and freshly ground pepper to taste

Whisk together the mustard and vinegar in a mixing bowl. Drizzle in the oils, whisking constantly to combine. Add salt and pepper to taste.

Strawberry Sauce

**1 pint basket hulled strawberries, or 1 10-ounce bag frozen
strawberries, thawed
3 tablespoons confectioner's sugar
1 teaspoon fresh lemon juice**

Combine all ingredients in a food processor or blender
and puree until smooth. Chill.

———●———

Sabayon of Fresh Fruit with Strawberry Sauce

**4 egg yolks
½ cup Sauternes dessert wine (or California Johannisberg
Riesling or German Alsatian Riesling or any dry white wine)
½ cup Grand Marnier
⅓ cup granulated sugar
2 cups fresh raspberries, strawberries or blueberries**

Combine the egg yolks, Sauternes, Grand Marnier and
sugar in a large metal bowl. Whisk until the mixture is smooth
and pale. A ribbon should form when the whisk is removed
from the mixture.

Place the bowl over a pan of simmering water. Be careful
that the bowl does not touch the hot water. Continue whisking
for about 10 minutes until the mixture thickens.

Pre-heat the broiler. Divide the berries into four individual
ovenproof gratin or custard dishes. Cover with sabayon. Place
the dishes on a baking sheet and broil for about one minute or
until just golden. Do not overcook. Before serving, each dish
should be drizzled with the strawberry sauce. Serves 4.

Michael Roberts

Trumps

1980–1992

*N*ew York may have had Donald and Ivana, but L.A. had Trumps. If the excessive eighties was the decade of the foodie, then Trumps was their Valhalla. Throughout the decade, the restaurant and bar located on the western reaches of Melrose Avenue helped define Los Angeles as a stylish restaurant city and was a continuing backdrop for the successful citizenry of West Hollywood. Trumps even looked different, vaguely Southwestern on the outside, ascetic on the inside. The concrete dining tables bore tiny exotic succulents and the walls provided a revolving display of paintings by L.A.'s artists and frequent patrons, such as Ed Ruscha and David Hockney.

The sophisticated, imaginative eatery opened at the beginning of the decade, and closed at the cusp of the following one, when the trend-conscious moved on to other gourmet pastures. But for years, members of L.A.'s ever-sophisticated creative community found the main attraction at Trumps to be its adventurous, ever-changing menu. Dishes such as plantains and caviar or quesadillas stuffed with grapes and brie served with sweet-pea guacamole were taken as seriously here as anything French in a sauce was anywhere else.

In the afternoons, Trumps offered a popular and terribly proper English-style tea with scones, cucumber sandwiches, sweets and sherry, all embellished with gentle harp music. Of course, if you wanted to, you could just sit at the bar and sip a Corona beer or a Perrier with lime.

Agents and publicists lunched there with their clients because it was flooded with sunlight and everyone could be seen, but tables were spread far enough apart to make eavesdropping difficult. At tea time, when the restaurant was at its quietest, Hollywood scribes conducted interviews along the banquettes. And legends of all generations dined there, from Elizabeth Taylor to Eddie Murphy and all his bodyguards, to Claudette Colbert and Lillian Hellman. Sam Shepard regularly ordered bourbon at the bar. Sally Field had a baby shower there.

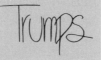

Famous chefs like Julia Child and James Beard thought so highly of Trumps' cuisine that they put the restaurant on their itinerary when visiting L.A. Former California governor Jerry Brown was an habitué during his term, and Senator Edward Kennedy often entertained there when he came through town. The restaurant tended to appeal more to Democrats, noted co-owner and chef Michael Roberts, while Republicans gathered at more conservative, Establishment-type

Plantains and Caviar

1 cup salad oil, or enough to fill a medium skillet
to a depth of 1 inch
3 medium-size plantains, peeled and diagonally cut
into ½-inch slices
4 heaped tablespoons sour cream or créme fraiche
4 heaped tablespoons Black Bean Puree (recipe below)
2 ounces black caviar
2 ounces golden caviar
¼ medium red onion, finely sliced tip to root

Heat oil in a medium skillet over medium heat to 375 degrees. Add the plantain slices, in batches if necessary, without crowding the skillet. Fry until lightly golden, about two minutes. Remove with a slotted spoon and repeat until all the slices are fried. Using the side of a cleaver or large chef's knife, gently flatten slices to a thickness of ⅜ inch. (Can be prepared to this point up to 8 hours in advance and kept covered on a plate at room temperature.) Re-fry slices until dark golden, another 2 to 3 minutes. Remove with a slotted spoon and drain on paper towels.

To serve, arrange 3 to 4 plantain slices on each plate. Spoon sour cream, black bean puree, and black and golden caviar over the slices. Garnish with slices of red onion. Serves 4 to 6.

————●————

Black Bean Puree

1 large carrot, roughly diced (about 1 cup)
1 medium onion, roughly diced (about ¾ cup)
1 small ham hock (3 ounces)
½ cup dried black beans
1 sprig fresh thyme or ½ teaspoon dried
2 cups water

Cook carrot, onion, ham hock, black beans, thyme and water in a small pot over low heat, covered, until beans are soft, 1 to 1½ hours. Drain. Discard ham hock and any remaining water.

Puree beans in processor until smooth, with slight chunks. Prepare beans no more than one day in advance. Reheat, in the top of a double boiler for 20 minutes, stirring occasionally.

places such as Chasen's or Jimmy's.

In 1992, Roberts, wanting to "express himself" elsewhere, decided to close up shop. Angelenos mourn the loss of his sautéed chicken with roasted garlic and candied lemon, plantains and caviar with black bean puree, and lemon nut cake with lemon custard.

Sautéed Chicken with Roasted Garlic and Candied Lemon

1 fryer chicken cut into 6 pieces
¼ cup olive oil
24 garlic cloves, unpeeled
2 cups canned low-sodium chicken broth
¼ cup fresh lemon juice
½ teaspoon salt
1 lemon, yellow zests only
⅓ cup sugar
½ cup water

Pre-heat oven to 425 degrees. Heat the oil in a 12-inch oven-proof skillet over high heat on top of the stove. Add the garlic cloves and sauté until the skins are a medium golden color. Remove and set aside the garlic. Add chicken and brown it on both sides.

Once the chicken is brown, return the garlic to the skillet. Without pouring off the cooking fat, add broth and juice. Sprinkle with salt, bring to a boil and place, uncovered, in the oven for 40 minutes, turning once.

Meanwhile, prepare the candied lemon. Cut the zest into ¼-inch strips and place in a small saucepan. Add sugar and water, bring to a boil over a medium heat and simmer gently, until nearly all the water is evaporated and zests look translucent and shiny. Strain zests, discard syrup and reserve zests on a plate.

Transfer skillet with chicken to stove top, place over high heat and reduce liquid until it has a shiny consistency. Arrange chicken pieces on a serving platter. Scrape garlic cloves and glaze over chicken. Garnish with candied zests. Serves 2 to 3.

Lemon Nut Cake

13 tablespoons unsalted butter (1 ½ sticks
plus 1 tablespoon)
1 cup sugar
5 eggs, separated
½ cup fresh bread crumbs
2 ½ cups chopped pistachios, blanched almonds or
pecans
½ teaspoon salt
4 cups lemon custard (recipe below)

Pre-heat oven to 375 degrees. Butter a deep 9-inch cake pan with 1 tablespoon butter. Combine remaining butter and sugar in a mixer and cream on medium speed until smooth. Add egg yolks one at a time. Then add the bread crumbs, 2 cups of the chopped nuts and mix. Place in a large mixing bowl and reserve.

Wash and completely dry the bowl of the mixer. Combine the salt and egg whites in the mixer and beat until stiff. Add one-third of the egg whites to the nut batter and mix to soften it. Place the rest of the egg whites on the batter and gently fold together. Pour batter into prepared cake pan. Place on the middle rack of the oven and bake for 30 minutes. When done, a wooden toothpick inserted in the cake should come out clean. Cool before unmolding.

Cut the cake in half horizontally. Spread a layer of lemon custard on it and reform the cake. Frost the entire outside with lemon custard and sprinkle with the remaining chopped nuts. Serve additional custard as an accompaniment. Serves 8.

Lemon Custard

5 eggs
5 egg yolks
2 cups sugar
1 cup fresh lemon juice
2 lemons, grated zest only
½ cup (1 stick) unsalted butter

Combine the eggs, egg yolks and sugar in a mixing bowl and beat until smooth. Add the lemon juice and zest and mix. Place the bowl over a pot of boiling water or in the top of a double boiler and stir vigorously with a wooden spoon until the mixture thickens. This mixture won't curdle, so don't worry about overcooking it a little. Remove the bowl and stir in the butter until it melts. Mixture will keep for up to three months in the refrigerator.

This custard can also be used for pie filling. This quantity will fill three 9-inch pie shells. To make a lemon custard pie, fill baked pie shell and bake the custard for 15 minutes at 375 degrees.

I N D E X

I N D E X

R e c i p e s

PHOTO CREDITS

We gratefully acknowledge the following for permission to reprint the photographs and images shown on the pages below:

Marc Wanamaker/Bison Archives:
Cover
p. 12 (The Cocoanut Grove)
p. 38 (Schwab's)
p. 40 (Don the Beachcomber)
p. 44 (Cock 'n Bull)
p. 48 (Players)
p. 52 (Romanoff's)
p. 56 (La Rue)
p. 70 (Cyrano)

Walter Scharfe:
p. 18 (The Brown Derby)

Ron Haver:
p. 22 (The Brown Derby)

I. Magnin:
p. 24 (Bullock's Wilshire Tea Room)

Los Angeles Public Library:
p. 13, 16 (The Cocoanut Grove)
p. 28 (Tick Tock Tea Room)
p. 35 (Perino's)

Milton and Kathie Weiss:
p. 30 (Mama Weiss)

Alan Berliner:
p. 74 (Ma Maison)
p. 80 (Trumps)

Menus and assorted memorabilia obtained from private collections.

BETTY GOODWIN

Betty Goodwin has written about the entertainment industry, style and the social scene in Los Angeles as a feature writer and a society editor for the *Los Angeles Herald Examiner*, and as a staff writer for the *Los Angeles Times*. She has contributed to many publications, including *Harper's Bazaar, Vogue, TV Guide, The New York Times* and *HG*; and continues to report on fashion and society for the *Los Angeles Times*. Her column, "Screen Style," on movie and television costumes, is carried by the Los Angeles Times Syndicate. She is the co-author of *L.A. Inside Out: The Architecture and Interiors of America's Most Colorful City* (Viking Studio). Ms. Goodwin is a native of Los Angeles.

ANGEL CITY PRESS

Angel City Press, Inc., was established in 1992, and is dedicated to the publication of high-quality nonfiction. Angel City Press is located in Santa Monica, California.

HOLLYWOOD DU JOUR

Hollywood du Jour was designed by Jeff Darnall of Darnall Design, Laguna Niguel, California. The book was produced on an Apple Macintosh IIci. Programs used include QuarkXPress, Adobe Illustrator and Adobe Photoshop. The font used in the body text is News Gothic 9 point; the font used in the chapter heads is Snell Bold. Both fonts are members of the Adobe type family. It was printed on a Harris 77-inch sheet-fed press at the Kingsport, Tennessee facility of Arcata Graphics Company.